CONTENTS

HERSHEY'S SWEET MILK CHOCOLATE KISSE

CAPPUCCINO-KISSED CHEESECAKE

MAKES 12 SERVINGS

1½ cups chocolate cookie crumbs

6 tablespoons butter or margarine, melted

1¼ cups HERSHEY'S MINI KISSESBRAND Milk Chocolates, divided

4 packages (8 ounces each) cream cheese, softened

⅔ cup sugar

3 eggs

⅓ cup milk

1 tablespoon instant espresso powder

¼ teaspoon ground cinnamon

ESPRESSO CREAM (recipe follows)

1 Heat oven to 350°F. Combine cookie crumbs and butter; press onto bottom and 1 inch up side of 9-inch springform pan.

2 Melt 1 cup chocolate pieces in small saucepan over low heat, stirring constantly. Combine cream cheese and sugar in large bowl, beating on medium speed of mixer until well blended. Add eggs, milk, espresso powder and cinnamon; beat on low speed until well blended. Add melted chocolate pieces; beat on medium 2 minutes. Spoon mixture into crust.

3 Bake 55 minutes. Remove from oven to wire rack. Cool 15 minutes; with knife, loosen cake from side of pan. Cool completely; remove side of pan. Cover; refrigerate at least 4 hours before serving.

4 To serve, garnish with ESPRESSO CREAM and remaining ¼ cup chocolates. Cover; refrigerate leftover cheesecake.

ESPRESSO CREAM

Beat ½ cup cold whipping cream, 2 tablespoons powdered sugar and 1 teaspoon instant espresso powder until stiff.

CLASSIC CHOCOLATE CREAM PIE

MAKES 8 SERVINGS

5 sections (½ ounce each) HERSHEY'S Unsweetened Chocolate Baking Bar, broken into pieces

3 cups milk, divided

1⅓ cups sugar

3 tablespoons all-purpose flour

3 tablespoons cornstarch

½ teaspoon salt

3 egg yolks

2 tablespoons butter or margarine

1½ teaspoons vanilla extract

1 baked (9-inch) pie crust, cooled, or 1 (9-inch) crumb crust

Sweetened whipped cream (optional)

1 Combine chocolate and 2 cups milk in medium saucepan; cook over medium heat, stirring constantly, just until mixture boils. Remove from heat and set aside.

2 Stir together sugar, flour, cornstarch and salt in medium bowl. Whisk remaining 1 cup milk into egg yolks in separate bowl; stir into sugar mixture. Gradually add to chocolate mixture. Cook over medium heat, whisking constantly, until mixture boils; boil and stir 1 minute. Remove from heat; stir in butter and vanilla.

3 Pour into prepared crust; press plastic wrap directly onto surface. Cool; refrigerate until well chilled. Top with whipped cream, if desired.

HERSHEY'S SWEET MILK CHOCOLATE KISSES

EASY MINI KISSES®
CHOCO-CHERRY PIE

MAKES ABOUT 8 SERVINGS

1 baked (9-inch) pie crust, cooled

1¾ cups (10-ounce package) HERSHEY'S MINI KISSESBRAND Milk Chocolates, divided

1½ cups miniature marshmallows

⅓ cup milk

1 cup (½ pint) cold whipping cream

1 can (21 ounces) cherry pie filling, chilled

Whipped topping

1 Prepare pie crust.

2 Place 1 cup chocolate pieces, marshmallows and milk in medium microwave-safe bowl. Microwave at MEDIUM (50%) 1½ to 2 minutes or until chocolate is softened and mixture is melted and smooth when stirred; cool completely.

3 Beat whipping cream in small bowl until stiff; fold into chocolate mixture. Spoon into prepared crust. Cover; refrigerate 4 hours or until firm.

4 Garnish top of pie with cherry pie filling, whipped topping and remaining chocolates just before serving. Refrigerate leftover pie.

HERSHEY'S SWEET MILK CHOCOLATE KISSE

HERSHEY'S® HUGS® AND KISSES® CANDIES CHOCOLATE CAKE

MAKES 12 SERVINGS

¾ cup (1½ sticks) butter or margarine, softened

1¾ cups sugar

2 eggs

1 teaspoon vanilla extract

2 cups all-purpose flour

¾ cup HERSHEY'S Cocoa or HERSHEY'S SPECIAL DARK Cocoa

1¼ teaspoons baking soda

½ teaspoon salt

1⅓ cups water

COCOA FUDGE FROSTING (recipe follows)

HERSHEY'S HUGSBRAND Candies or HERSHEY'S KISSESBRAND Milk Chocolates

1 Heat oven to 350°F. Grease and flour 13×9×2-inch baking pan.

2 Beat butter and sugar in large bowl until fluffy. Add eggs and vanilla; beat 1 minute on medium speed of mixer. Stir together flour, cocoa, baking soda and salt; add alternately with water to butter mixture, beating until well blended. Pour batter into prepared pan.

3 Bake 40 to 45 minutes or until wooden pick inserted in center comes out clean. Cool 10 minutes; remove from pan to wire rack. Cool completely. Frost with COCOA FUDGE FROSTING. Remove wrappers from candies; garnish cake as desired with candies.

HERSHEY'S SWEET MILK CHOCOLATE KISSE

COCOA FUDGE FROSTING

MAKES ABOUT 2½ CUPS FROSTING

½ cup (1 stick) butter or margarine

½ cup HERSHEY'S Cocoa or HERSHEY'S SPECIAL DARK Cocoa

3⅔ cups (1 pound) powdered sugar

⅓ cup milk, heated

1 teaspoon vanilla extract

Melt butter in small saucepan over low heat; stir in cocoa. Cook, stirring constantly, until mixture thickens slightly. Remove from heat; pour into small mixer bowl. Add powdered sugar alternately with warm milk, beating to spreading consistency. Stir in vanilla. Spread frosting while warm.

HERSHEY'S® MINI KISSES® MILK CHOCOLATE PEANUT BUTTER COOKIES

MAKES 18 COOKIES

¼ cup (½ stick) butter or margarine, softened

¼ cup REESE'S Creamy Peanut Butter

¼ cup granulated sugar

¼ cup packed light brown sugar

1 egg

½ teaspoon vanilla extract

⅔ cup all-purpose flour

¼ teaspoon baking soda

⅛ teaspoon salt

1¾ cups (10-ounce package) HERSHEY'S MINI KISSES BRAND Milk Chocolates

1 Heat oven to 350°F. Lightly grease cookie sheet or line with parchment paper.

2 Beat butter and peanut butter in large bowl on medium speed of electric mixer until creamy. Gradually add granulated sugar and brown sugar, beating until well mixed. Add egg and vanilla; beat until light and fluffy. Stir together flour, baking soda and salt; add to butter mixture, beating until well blended. Stir in chocolates. Drop batter by rounded tablespoons onto prepared cookie sheet.

3 Bake 10 to 12 minutes or until lightly browned. Cool slightly; remove from cookie sheet to wire rack. Cool completely.

HUGS® & KISSES®
CRESCENTS
MAKES 8 CRESCENTS

1 package (8 ounces) refrigerated crescent dinner rolls
24 HERSHEY'S KISSESBRAND Milk Chocolates or
**   HERSHEY'S HUGSBRAND Candies**
Powdered sugar

1 Heat oven to 375°F. Separate dough into 8 triangles. Remove wrappers from chocolates.

2 Place 2 chocolates at center of wide end of each triangle; place an additional chocolate on top of other two pieces. Starting at wide end, roll to opposite point; pinch edges to seal. Place rolls, pointed side down, on ungreased cookie sheet. Curve into crescent shape.

3 Bake 10 minutes or until lightly browned. Cool slightly; sift with powdered sugar. Serve warm.

NOTE
Leftover crescents can be reheated
in microwave for a few seconds.

KISSED PRETZEL S'MORES

MAKE AS DESIRED

Small pretzels (twisted)
Miniature marshmallows

HERSHEY'S KISSESBRAND
Milk Chocolates

1 Heat oven to 350°F. Line cookie sheet with parchment paper or foil.

2 Place 1 pretzel for each pretzel s'more desired on prepared sheet. Top each pretzel with 3 marshmallows and another pretzel.

3 Bake 4 to 5 minutes or until marshmallows soften and begin to puff. Remove from oven and gently press KISSES chocolates on each top pretzel. Allow treats to sit several minutes in order for chocolate pieces to melt enough to adhere to pretzels and to soften slightly. Treats are best if eaten while chocolate piece is soft.

KISSES® COCONUT MACAROON BLOSSOMS

MAKES ABOUT 48 COOKIES

⅓ cup butter or margarine, softened

1 package (3 ounces) cream cheese, softened

¾ cup sugar

1 egg yolk

2 teaspoons almond extract

2 teaspoons orange juice

1¼ cups all-purpose flour

2 teaspoons baking powder

¼ teaspoon salt

5 cups MOUNDS Sweetened Coconut Flakes, divided

48 HERSHEY'S KISSESBRAND Milk Chocolates

1 Beat butter, cream cheese and sugar with electric mixer on medium speed in large bowl until well blended. Add egg yolk, almond extract and orange juice; beat well. Stir together flour, baking powder and salt; gradually add to butter mixture. Stir in 3 cups coconut. Cover; refrigerate 1 hour or until firm enough to handle. Meanwhile, remove wrappers from chocolates.

2 Heat oven to 350°F.

3 Shape dough into 1-inch balls; roll in remaining 2 cups coconut. Place on ungreased cookie sheet.

4 Bake 10 to 12 minutes or until lightly browned. Remove from oven; immediately press chocolate piece into center of each cookie. Cool 1 minute. Carefully remove to wire rack and cool completely.

KISSES® PEANUT BUTTER BLOSSOMS

MAKES ABOUT 48 COOKIES

48 HERSHEY'S KISSESBRAND
Milk Chocolates

¾ cup REESE'S Creamy
Peanut Butter

½ cup shortening

⅓ cup granulated sugar

⅓ cup packed light brown
sugar

1 egg

2 tablespoons milk

1 teaspoon vanilla extract

1½ cups all-purpose flour

1 teaspoon baking soda

½ teaspoon salt

⅓ cup additional granulated
sugar for rolling

1 Heat oven to 375°F. Remove wrappers from chocolates.

2 Beat peanut butter and shortening with electric mixer on medium speed in large bowl until well blended. Add ⅓ cup granulated sugar and brown sugar; beat until fluffy. Add egg, milk and vanilla; beat well. Stir together flour, baking soda and salt; gradually beat into peanut butter mixture.

3 Shape dough into 1-inch balls. Roll in additional granulated sugar; place on ungreased cookie sheet.

4 Bake 8 to 10 minutes or until lightly browned. Immediately press a chocolate into center of each cookie; cookies will crack around edges. Remove to wire racks and cool completely.

MELTAWAY BROWNIE BITES

MAKES ABOUT 48 BROWNIE BITES

48 Any flavor HERSHEY'S KISSESBRAND Chocolates or HERSHEY'S HUGSBRAND Candies

⅔ cup butter or margarine, softened

1¼ cups granulated sugar

1 tablespoon water

1 teaspoon vanilla extract

2 eggs

1½ cups all-purpose flour

½ cup HERSHEY'S Cocoa or HERSHEY'S SPECIAL DARK Cocoa

½ teaspoon salt

¼ teaspoon baking soda

Powdered sugar

1 Remove wrappers from chocolates; place in freezer while preparing and baking cookies.

2 Beat butter, granulated sugar, water and vanilla in large bowl on medium speed of mixer until well blended. Add eggs; beat well. Stir together flour, cocoa, salt and baking soda. Gradually add to sugar mixture, beating on low speed until blended. Cover; refrigerate dough about 2 hours or until firm enough to handle.

3 Heat oven to 350°F. Line 48 small muffin cups (1¾ inches in diameter) with paper or foil baking cups or lightly spray with vegetable cooking spray. Shape dough into 1-inch balls; place in prepared muffin cups.

4 Bake 11 to 13 minutes or until cookie surface is set. Cookies will appear soft and moist. Do not overbake. Cool about 5 minutes on wire rack. Dust cookie tops with powdered sugar. Press frozen chocolate piece into surface of each cookie. Cool completely in pan on wire rack.

MINI KISSES® COCONUT MACAROON BARS

MAKES 16 BARS

3¾ cups MOUNDS Sweetened Coconut Flakes

¾ cup sugar

¼ cup all-purpose flour

¼ teaspoon salt

3 egg whites

1 egg, slightly beaten

1 teaspoon almond extract

1¾ cups (10-ounce package) HERSHEY'S MINI KISSESBRAND Milk Chocolates, divided

1 Heat oven to 350°F. Lightly grease 9-inch square baking pan.

2 Stir together coconut, sugar, flour and salt in large bowl. Add egg whites, egg and almond extract; stir until well blended. Set aside 2 tablespoons chocolates; stir remaining chocolates into coconut mixture. Spread mixture in prepared pan, covering all chocolate pieces with coconut mixture.

3 Bake 35 minutes or until lightly browned. Remove from oven to wire rack. Immediately sprinkle reserved chocolates over surface, pressing down lightly. Cool completely in pan on wire rack.

4 Cover with foil; allow to stand at room temperature about 8 hours or overnight. Cut into bars.

VARIATION

Place reserved chocolates and ½ teaspoon shortening (do not use butter, margarine, spread or oil) in small microwave-safe bowl. Microwave at MEDIUM (50%) 1 minute; stir. If necessary, microwave an additional 10 seconds at a time, stirring after each heating, just until chocolates are melted and mixture is smooth when stirred. Drizzle over top.

SECRET KISSES® COOKIES

MAKES ABOUT 36 COOKIES

1 cup (2 sticks) butter or margarine, softened

½ cup granulated sugar

1 teaspoon vanilla extract

1¾ cups all-purpose flour

1 cup finely chopped walnuts or almonds

36 HERSHEY'S KISSESBRAND Milk Chocolates or HERSHEY'S KISSESBRAND Milk Chocolates with Almonds

Powdered sugar for rolling

1 Beat butter, granulated sugar and vanilla with electric mixer on medium speed in large bowl until fluffy. Add flour and walnuts; beat on low speed of mixer until well blended. Cover; refrigerate 1 to 2 hours or until dough is firm enough to handle.

2 Remove wrappers from chocolates. Heat oven to 375°F. Using about 1 tablespoon dough for each cookie, shape dough around each chocolate; roll in hand to make ball. (Be sure to cover each chocolate piece completely.) Place on ungreased cookie sheet.

3 Bake 10 to 12 minutes or until cookies are set but not browned. Cool slightly; remove to wire rack. While still slightly warm, roll in powdered sugar. Cool completely. Store in tightly covered container. Roll again in powdered sugar just before serving.

VARIATION

Sift together 1 tablespoon HERSHEY'S Cocoa with ⅓ cup powdered sugar. Roll warm cookies in cocoa mixture.

TINY MINI KISSES® PEANUT BUTTER BLOSSOMS

MAKES ABOUT 14 DOZEN COOKIES

¾ cup REESE'S Creamy Peanut Butter

½ cup shortening

⅓ cup granulated sugar

⅓ cup packed light brown sugar

1 egg

3 tablespoons milk

1 teaspoon vanilla extract

1½ cups all-purpose flour

½ teaspoon baking soda

½ teaspoon salt

⅓ cup additional granulated sugar for rolling

1⅓ cups HERSHEY'S MINI KISSESBRAND Milk Chocolates

1 Heat oven to 350°F.

2 Beat peanut butter and shortening in large bowl with mixer until well blended. Add ⅓ cup granulated sugar and brown sugar; beat well. Add egg, milk and vanilla; beat until fluffy. Stir together flour, baking soda and salt; gradually add to peanut butter mixture, beating until blended. Shape into ½-inch balls. Roll in granulated sugar; place on ungreased cookie sheet.

3 Bake 5 to 6 minutes or until set. Immediately press chocolate into center of each cookie. Remove from cookie sheet to wire rack. Cool completely.

VARIATION

For larger cookies, shape dough into 1-inch balls. Roll in granulated sugar. Place on ungreased cookie sheet. Bake 10 minutes or until set. Immediately place 3 chocolate pieces in center of each cookie, pressing down slightly. Remove from cookie sheet to wire rack. Cool completely.

TWO GREAT TASTES PUDDING PARFAITS

MAKES 6 SERVINGS

1 package (6-serving size) vanilla cook & serve pudding and pie filling mix*

3½ cups milk

1 cup REESE'S Peanut Butter Chips

1 cup HERSHEY'S MINI KISSESBRAND Milk Chocolates

Whipped topping (optional)

Additional HERSHEY'S MINI KISSESBRAND Milk Chocolates or grated chocolate

Do not use instant pudding mix.

1 Combine pudding mix and 3½ cups milk in large heavy saucepan (rather than amount listed in package directions). Cook over medium heat, stirring constantly, until mixture comes to a full boil. Remove from heat; divide hot mixture between 2 heatproof medium bowls.

2 Immediately stir peanut butter chips into mixture in one bowl and chocolates into second bowl. Stir both mixtures until chips are melted and mixture is smooth. Cool slightly, stirring occasionally.

3 Alternately layer peanut butter and chocolate mixtures in parfait dishes, wine glasses or dessert dishes. Place plastic wrap directly onto surface of each dessert; refrigerate about 6 hours. Garnish with whipped topping, if desired, and chocolate pieces.